C000271985

ephebos

kostya tsolakis

ignit**i**onpress

for my parents

First published in 2020
by **ignition**press
Oxford Brookes Poetry Centre
Oxford Brookes University
OX3 0BP

Cover design: Flora Hands, Carline Creative

A CIP record for this book is available from the British Library

ISBN 978-1-9161328-7-0

Contents

Ολίγες ώρες πριν πεθάνει, κάτι
ψιθύρισε για «οικίαν», για «πολύ γέροντας γονείς».

Κωνσταντίνος Π. Καβάφης, «Εις το επίνειον»

Bathroom in an Athens Suburb, 1994

All I have are catalogues
from archaeological museums –
page after page of glossy athletes,
gods and heroes, in bronze
or marble, some missing limbs,
noses, heads, others full-bodied.
At first, I'm happy to look,
flick through their fractured perfections.
Soon, growing bolder, I will them
off their pedestals, let them stretch
after millennia of holding
celebrated poses, grant them hearts,
a pulse, sinew and permeable skin.
Grateful, they let me touch them.
Trembling, I examine the scars
dug by the ploughs of farmers
and fishermen's anchors. I close my eyes,
smell the earth that clings
to the tangled hair of those found
in muddy fields, the hint of iodine
in the sweat of those raised
from ancient shipwrecks, ignore
the ochre scent of my mother's
cosmetics on the wicker shelf.
No one will knock and ask
what I'm doing locked behind
this door. I don't want to come out,
though as summer nears,
it gets harder and harder
to breathe.

Antlers

I catch my father admiring them
on the boys who live in our block,
boys who bellow at each other
on the basketball court, who fill
their cars with petrol, or work
in tight blue jeans at the taverna

in the park. My schoolmates
carry theirs with pride – true bone
rising from stiff-gelled heads. I know
my neck could not stand the weight.
Vitamins and vats of milk
can't make mine grow. Still small

as thumbs, even coating them
in honey mixed with blood
will not work. I watch the boys
strut around the schoolyard,
how they always compare
scars, size each other up –

how a playful slap in the face
escalates into rutting, into
twisting violence, pulled-up shirts
exposing lean, winter-pale
waists, sweating bodies
and antlers intertwined.

Evenings of Winter, 1995

Inspired by my grandmother's *Lives of the Martyrs*,
I draw crucifixions, beheadings, stonings.
Catherine on the wheel.
Sebastian taking the arrows.

I spend hours sketching them
in the Byzantine manner
on heavy matte paper:
saints, angels and apostles.

Outlines firm in black felt-tip,
colours filled in vividly with ink.
Tongue sticking out in concentration, I'm careful
not to let them bleed into each other.

I love to draw Cain killing Abel,
Moses taking off his shoes,
David embracing Jonathan,
beautiful Absalom washing his hair.

Every now and then, my father checks on me.
You'll ruin your eyes, he says,
like Saint Paraskevi
who holds hers in a plate.

I carry on with creation
in the halo of my desk lamp,
taking great care as I draw naked Adam
receiving the apple from Eve.

First Time

I wear the blue Versace polo shirt,
one size too big, my mother bought me.

We meet in Thissio, sit outside
a bar by the Temple of Hephaestus.

He looks different from the pic he sent –
balder, heavier. But he has a smooth voice,
the kind they use in milk or yoghurt adverts.
I lie about my age.

I have a Moscow Mule in a coral bottle.
He drinks something in a heavy-bottomed glass.
We talk about our summer plans.

A taxi takes us to a place north of Omonia Square.
In the dark hotel reception, he pays
5,000 drachmas. A blue note. I don't contribute.

Even with the window open, the room stifles.
On a tray, laid out like wedding rings,
two condoms.
He keeps the light off.

I'd expected lovemaking to be
a soft, easy affair –
a seaside room,
the scent of lemons,
lapping waves.

Instead, this angular, stinky wrestle,
and his voice turning childish,
he calls me *baby*
as we soak the bedlinen.

We dress in the dark.
We don't kiss goodnight.
If there was blood on the sheet,
it isn't the sort tradition likes
presented from a balcony.

Photographs

On balconies, in sunlit rooms, embracing
relatives I never met, holding long-dead pets,

my parents' youth is kept in the living room
in a wooden chest. Deckled prints no bigger

than my palm, formal studio portraits
and light-starved slides span monochrome

decades, peaking in Kodak Gold right before
I was born. Again and again my parents are caught

ignorant of me. Dad, nearing ninety now, his mouth
a sparrow that no longer flies. How can he be

the smart lieutenant Mum has yet to fall for,
his uniform a brilliant white he can't be trusted

with today? Mum, her eyes dimmed by limitations
and disappointment. Is she the girl, stem-thin

in a little black dress, gazed at by pomaded suitors?
Even then she felt like a displaced floor tile,

but in that girl's beautiful, composed face,
there's no hint of the anxious woman watching now

in terror, as the cold light of life without him
leaks in, like a new development, from under the door.

Conversion

and the wife see that she reverence her husband.

Ephesians 5:33

Cured in the church my parents were married in,
I was made to kneel on the marble floor,
face the gilded iconostasis for hours
as chants and swigs of holy water rooted out
the homosexual demons from my body. The painted saints
that witnessed my translation later watched over
my union with you, dear wife – their cool expressions,
just like yours, gave nothing away. Mother smiled,
the priest chanted: *η δε γυνή ίνα φοβήται τον άνδρα.*
You stepped lightly on my toes. Was this her idea?
The wreath on my head felt surprisingly heavy. I wore
my father's velvet suit, tight over my chest and under
the armpits; downed too many raki shots at the reception.

It's been a year. Are you my ideal match? Mother
certainly thinks so. Unlike me, you learned how to drive,
never gave up on your German, read Balzac and Zola
in the French, had a stint in the diplomatic corps. Men
give you the eye in the street. I pretend to mind
but can't make myself. You spend a lot of time
with my mother, hanging off each other's lips. Just now,
in the kitchen, you giggled like girls with a crush. I try
to join you, but you shoo me away. *We're talking
women stuff*, you laugh. I sit on the steps that lead
down to the garden, smoking. I picked up smoking
recently. The apple tree is looking worse for wear.
It hasn't rained since we got married.

totality

solar eclipse, Crete, 11 August 1999

the car's an incubator/ even
with the windows down/ squashed
in the back of the boxy rental/ I'm taller
than both my parents/ radio says/ today
will hit 40°C/ we're too far south/ to wow
at the diamond ring/ for the sky to dim/
pacing the water's edge/ in the brooding
heat/ the clammy nylon of my swim shorts
clings/ I kick and kick/ the breathless
sea/ next month/ I can learn to drive/ buy
alcohol/ gamble/ next month/ I'll find
my cool release/ in the shadows
of England's parks/ next month/
next month/

My Visitors

after Andreas Angelakis

Morning after kicking morning
I carry a stomachful of boys
my eyes devoured whole
on dance floors long emptied and torn down

Seeds that keep in my gut
their anise taste repeats
I choke
        Look how grey my chin is now

Nights they sprout back into boy
unfurl through my belly button
causing only slight discomfort

They sit on the edge of the bath
as I brush my teeth and fret
over the blood-letting in the sink

They pluck old paperbacks from my shelves
flick through them blankly
postcards from exes drop from the pages

Under the duvet
they slip in beside me
lukewarm hair gel   nicotine   dry ice

In the Kitchen with Dad

For dinner, Dad has paximadia,
the spicy green peppers he likes grilled,
a portion of cheese and a glass of red.
Mum now buys his wine from Lidl.
It's cheap, but very good, Dad says.

Are you happy in England? he asks.
Feigning satisfaction with my usual answer,
he goes on telling me stories of Pat Pattle,
the RAF pilot he's reading about.
The Nazis shot him to pieces, aged twenty-six.
The Greeks have forgotten him, Dad says.

Another glass and Dad recites Homer
in Classical Greek, which I don't understand,
then hums a German drinking song
his mother sang to him before the war.
By his third glass, Dad's plate is empty.
The untimely dead of his life
have gathered around the table.
Wiping his eyes, Dad says:
Be patient with your mother,
I deal with her all day.

Fragments of Emails from My Mother in 2011

the year I came out to my parents
the peak of the Greek financial crisis

07/01/2011 18:02   Kostiko/ only when you have a family and child/ will you understand how much we miss you/

08/01/2011 17:07   I keep asking the questions/ you never answer/ I know nothing about you/

13/01/2011 11:51   the cats are fine/ Barbarossa sometimes pees inside the house/

15/01/2011 12:32   I found out from Papa that you're well/ you didn't ask after me/

26/01/2011 14:26   Kostiko/ I went to church/ I hope god listens/

30/01/2011 12:43   we call and call/ you never pick up/ we must chat sometime or else/ all alone here we'll get depressed/

04/02/2011 16:11   Skype me/ I'll show you the cats/

11/02/2011 20:12   can you see I'm calling you on Skype/ and won't answer/ or am I dumb?/

09/03/2011 17:59   thank you for remembering me/ you made me very happy/ I'm sorry I cried so much/ when I hear your voice/ I get emotional/ your dad forgot me/

03/04/2011 10:47   we miss your voice/ your laughter/ your arguing/

02/05/2011 21:43   we had guests/ I couldn't talk in front of them/ I'm here for you/ I'd love you even if you murdered someone/

02/05/2011 23:39   you made me happy with your presence/ in my life/

05/05/2011 20:40   what's new?/ the weather's awful here/

02/06/2011 15:43   Kostiko/ don't be sad/ look out for what's best in your life/

11/07/2011 16:24   you won't answer/ I forget what it is I've asked you/

25/07/2011 20:51   answer me/ when can we talk on Skype?/

03/08/2011 14:11   we had Barbarossa neutered/ he is very sad/

28/08/2011 21:22   are you in Spain?/ in Germany?/ give me a missed call/ so I know you're well/

04/09/2011 20:11   still waiting for your call/ why are you avoiding us?/ are you that busy?/

18/09/2011 18:43   Blanche is a very calm cat/ the best of them all/ Barbarossa runs off to the empty plot across the street/ he responds when we call him/ comes over for a bit/ but he lives there now/

24/09/2011 20:36   Kostiko/ Yiayia was feeling terrible yesterday/ she said you didn't call her/ I don't know if you'll ever see her again/

06/10/2011 18:19   you only ever call me/ to tell me your pain/

12/10/2011 17:45   strikes all the time here/ a bomb went off near our old shop/ thank god no one died/ when will I see you on Skype?/

09/11/2011 20:11   Kostiko/ you've vanished/ send me news/ please/

18/11/2011 16:25   Kostiko/ the time has come for me to do something about your room/ it's clear to me you'll never live in Greece/ and I look at your stuff every day/ the way you left them/ I feel sad/ and miss you even more/

21/11/2011 20:26   call your cousin/ it's her name day/

07/12/2011 12:36   I have no friends/ your yiayia loves your auntie more than me/ though Sophie always has a go at her/

08/12/2011 17:04   don't be soft/ don't let your emotions affect your work/

11/12/2011 13:26   we went to a birthday party/ Papa got emotional/ he misses you/ but really we are happy that you live abroad/ in a serious country/

19/12/2011 18:11   now you're a grown man/ I want you to tell me what you think/ about my character/

20/12/2011 22:24   you have become an Englishman/

21/12/2011 21:22   you were good at everything/ we told you all the time/ you chose your own path/

28/12/2011 20:16   Kostiko/ there was blood in Barbarossa's pee/ all through the holidays/ we had no option/ I buried him in the garden myself/

30/12/2011 21:18   Kostiko/ you've vanished again/ you work every day/ you're out weekends/ when's our turn to hear your voice?/

Nobody

My host, whose threshold I crossed
half an hour ago, who offered me a drink
in a plastic tumbler, who asked me to talk him
through my tattoos, is turning me onto
my stomach. Kissing my back, he whispers
his plea. Again I laugh it off. *Please,*
his voice is saying, but his body's telling me
the time to negotiate is over. I discover
what it's like to be a flower pressed
under a dozen volumes on a drawn-out
civil war. He spit-hooks himself inside me.
Lightning bolts up my spine, splits me.
And each half will seek the other forever.
I'm left with the smell of sweat
and poppers gone flat on his pillow,
a muddied running shoe in the corner. I'm split
into before and after photos. Twenty-eight days
of hard-to-swallow pills, in case he spilled
a new kind of life into me.
No compassionate god will come
turn me into something small and winged
to slip away.

Hounds

You never barked or growled,
showed no desire to lick my face.
The sight of leg didn't excite you.
I stroked your heads, offered you
treats. Your sparkless eyes
and stiffened tails gave me no sign.
Like satellites, you followed
everywhere I went. I took you
to the parks I liked, we walked
the walks I loved. People stared,
never approached us – you terrified
their children – but, for me,
your mute companionship would do.
I said all kinds of things to you.
I talked about my family, secrets,
desires. At heart I thought
the honesty in my words
would charm you into love
like some enchanted lyre.
Maybe my voice began to grate
or proved how soft I was.
Whatever the cause – without
a sound you tore me up like dough.
Didn't stop until all that was left
was bone.

Naming It

The cause of the disorder is unknown. Researchers call it A.I.D., for acquired immunodeficiency disease, or GRID, for gay-related immunodeficiency.

The New York Times, 11 May 1982

We sweat all night, soak
our beds, fill wards, spill
out of hospitals, slurry
the roads. We die
under dripping awnings,
in tavern yards, in barns.
Our cries cut deeply
into the skin of hearing.
Doctors name it after us.
Kids add it to the things
you catch in tag. They say God
brought it down, that it came
in a foreign ship, that you catch it
shaking hands, sharing cups.
People in high places get it,
holy men, teachers, national treasures
after a hundred deaths on stage.
Those who haven't, rush past us, bolt
their doors, seal their heavy windows.
Leaders tell us they are *on it*,
that doctors spend all day
and night looking for a cure.
But really they are busy with diplomacy,
with how the nation looks abroad.
And all the while, our shrouded corpses
carpet the steps of government,
and we run out of paper
to list our dead.

The Case of Vangelis Yakoumakis

after Cavafy

In this muddy ditch, overlooked by naked branches,
lies the decomposing body of Vangelis, a Cretan.

He studied at the dairy academy nearby. Missing
for thirty-seven days, he was sighted all over Greece

at once. The press described him as *sensitive, a loner.*
Bullies slapped him while he ate. When he showered,

they turned the water off. Someone kicked him down
a flight of stairs. Someone locked him in a closet,

made him sing for hours. Then the video: six sniggering
guys piling on top of him. Thousands heard Vangelis beg,

Please stop, you're hurting me. His voice smaller than an olive.
All this was recorded. So was the knife found at his side.

What's lost are his features, the smooth flesh on his cheek,
where his mother would kiss him goodbye.

The Watch

I sold it, got less than I hoped,
enough to last me two months, three if careful.
Loveless, sleepless weekends on strangers' lube-greased sofa beds.

I promised Dad I'd give it to the son
I'd name after him.
The phantom shackle around my wrist.

I catch glimpses of it in old photographs,
shuffle through them quickly,
the images ticking against my fingertips.

My surname means *one-armed* or *handicapped*.
Unkind nickname turned family name.
Dad always gave money to the one-armed beggar at the traffic lights.

I think of him, the village cripple from how-many hundred years ago.
I carry his Y chromosome.
At my birth, the surgeon cried out *Αρτιμελής!*

The dealer said the clasp would have to be changed.
A.Δ.T. engraved in beautiful cursive.
A hundred quid struck off for each of Dad's initials.

Sparrow

The day before the royal wedding,
rainbow flags jostled for air with
Union Jack bunting. Hurrying up
Old Compton Street, I phoned my father.
From neon posters, near-naked boys invited me
to all-weekend-long parties at the clubs.
Every stranger I passed looked happier than me.

I cried so much the night before.
Said perhaps I can send my yiayia:
two floors down from their flat,
she could tell them over breakfast.
I could picture her doing it: pink
dressing gown over her nightdress,
light-footed in her fluffy slippers.
The angel with the message.
If it came out of her mouth
like a velvet ribbon, surely
they couldn't turn their faces from it?
My mother looking at her scrambled eggs
as if they were vomit.

I said to Dad we could no longer live like this.
And in my ear Dad said, *It's all right*,
in the careful voice I'd heard him use
when talking to sparrows –
those curious little things, so easy to frighten,
that would perch, hollow-boned, on the railing
as he tended his delicate balcony plants.

Forefathers

The sun has set. It's mild,
but the square is empty.
I sit outside Rooster with a beer.
Inside, the bar is packed.
Boys come in and out,
greet their friends,
a kiss on each cheek.
The way they dress,
they look straight out of Dalston.
But through the glass
I can tell they're Greek
from how their lips move.
Do my lips expose me too?

Sporting neat moustaches,
Athenian boys resemble
their handsome grandfathers
but with earrings, high-tops
and strict black fringes.

Perched above the awning,
a neon cockerel inspects the square.
Twenty-four centuries ago, a rooster
or hare was a love gift
from bearded gentlemen
to smooth-chinned ephebes. Today,
it's the offer of a lighter, a look.

My grandfather's shop
was a five-minute walk from here,
down Aiolou Street,
near the Tower of the Winds.
He was a textile printer
with ashen curly hair,
clean-shaven. Liked women –
liked women a lot.

Someone Else's Child

On 21 September 2018, 33-year-old LGBTQ+ activist and drag performer Zak Kostopoulos was brutally beaten up by two men after entering a jewellery shop in central Athens. In video footage, police officers are seen to be violently arresting Zak, and one officer is seen kicking him. According to the forensic report, Zak died from the multiple injuries he sustained.

I undress, watched over by medals for bravery
and life achievement awards in Dad's study, sleep
on mismatched sheets in the new sofa bed – stiff
mattress unyielding to my shape. Square-jawed,
great-uncle Grigoris – army coat too big
for him, battle-muddied boots – stares straight
out of his thumb-smudged picture frame.

Morning. The mountains that penned in
my childhood are covered in snow. Dad mutters
in the hallway: *The Archangel has abandoned me.*
He keeps silent over lunch, eyes fixed
on his soup, as though afraid he's close
to using up his allocated words. Walking to the café,
he hands me his cane, won't take my arm.

The bow-tied waiter shakes Dad's hand, calls
me by my dead half-brother's name. I don't
correct him, neither does Dad. Untouched,
Dad's espresso grows cold. Now and then a spinning
light speeds by, washes his face a watery blue.
So much police, I say. Dad doesn't respond. I want
to tell him how, minutes from here, someone else's

child, made of the same material as me, was made
immaterial. How buffed boots, ordered to *prevent*
and *quell*, judged him a bone-snatching stray, infected
with god-knows. How they pinned him, hand-cuffed,
against the rough, uneven pavement, kicked his heart
in. A Friday lunchtime in this city. But your weary
expression, Father, clamps the words to my throat.

Athenian Light

I was born into it
in late September,
when it's sweet and hued at sunset
like the seeded flesh of figs.
Smog meddled with it,
hanging over Athens
like bad history.

Growing up,
what use was lyrical light
when stuck two hours every day
in an airless school bus,
gum spat in my hair
by the back row boys?

After half a lifetime in England,
I bathe in it by a rooftop pool,
swallows above me
like musical notes,
the broken jawline
of the Parthenon within sight,
and I love how it brings out
the veins in marble
and the arms of men.

I watch the child in the pool
learn how to swim,
wearing, just like I did,
orange inflatable arm bands,
remember my father's insistence
that you can drown
even in the clearest light.

Acknowledgments

The Greek epigraph to this pamphlet is taken from the 1918 poem by Constantine P. Cavafy «Εις το επίνειον». In English, its title has been translated as 'In the Harbor-Town' (Edmund Keeley and Philip Sherrard), 'In this Port' (Evan Jones) and 'Safe Haven' (Daniel Mendelsohn), among others. The lines, as translated by Edmund Keeley and Philip Sherrard, are:

> A few hours before dying he whispered something
> about 'home,' about 'very old parents.'

I wish to thank the editors of the following magazines where poems from this pamphlet first found a home: *Ambit*, *Anthropocene*, *The Fenland Reed*, *Magma*, *Pamenar Press Online Magazine*, *perverse*, *The Scores*, *Stone of Madness Press*, *Strix*, *Wasafiri* and *whynow*.

I am grateful to Jackie Kay for awarding 'Photographs' First Place in the 2019 Oxford Brookes International Poetry Competition (EAL category). 'Conversion' received a Special Commendation and 'In the Kitchen with Dad' was shortlisted in the same competition.

'Hounds' was Highly Commended in the York Literature Festival/ YorkMix Poetry Competition 2018, judged by Andrew McMillan.

'Naming It' was included in the New River Press 2019 anthology *WHEN THEY START TO LOVE YOU AS A MACHINE YOU SHOULD RUN.*

'Athenian Light' was showcased online as part of the ten-poet shortlist for the Primers mentoring scheme in 2017, run by The Poetry School, London, and Nine Arches Press.

Thank you to Romalyn Ante, Matthew Beavers, Jim English, Katie Griffiths, Stephen Guy-Bray, Seán Hewitt, Alice Hiller, Andrew McMillan, Astra Papachristodoulou and Paul Stephenson for your generous feedback, friendship and support. My thanks, also, to Rebecca Tamás for your critical eye and insightful advice.

To Heidi Williamson – thank you for your ongoing mentoring and friendship. I wouldn't be the poet I am without you.

A big thank you to the **ignition**press team.

To Tim – with all my love.